THE ESSENTIAL VALUES OF BUSINESS NETWORKING GROUPS

Connecting the Dots and
building businesses

Patrick K Teak

TFP

Thankyou to all the business networks who have allowed me to be a member. Your contributions have been instrumental to my success.

I would like to express my sincere gratitude to my business networks for the opportunities you have provided me and the valuable relationships we have built together.

Thank you for being an important part of my business growth and development.

CONTENTS

INTRODUCTION

In today's fast-paced business world, networking has become an essential part of building and growing a successful business.

Business networking is not just about meeting new people and making connections.

It is also about building meaningful relationships and creating a community of like-minded professionals, who can help each other achieve their goals, and business owners who are willing to pass the baton down to the next wave of entrepreneurs.

There are many values we need to uphold in business networking. In this ebook, we will explore the essential values to succeeding in business networking and how they can help you grow your business.

CHAPTER 1: CONNECTING THE DOTS

There were two people who were only two degrees of separation apart. Their names were Tom and Sarah.

Tom was a successful businessman who had made his fortune through a chain of popular cafes that he had started. He was a well-respected member of the community and often gave back by volunteering his time and resources to local charities and a local business networking group.

Sarah, on the other hand, was a struggling artist who was trying to make a name for herself in the art world. She had recently moved to New Zealand from Europe and was finding it difficult to break into the local art scene.

One day, a mutual friend introduced her to a neighbour who took her along to a business networking group and introduced Tom and Sarah. Tom was impressed by Sarah's talent and tenacity and offered to help her if he could. He had a friend give her a space in one of his restaurants to showcase her artwork and Tom organized an exhibition for her at his son's cafe.

The exhibition was a huge success, and Sarah's artwork was sold out within weeks. Tom was thrilled for her and continued to support her by introducing her to influential people in the business and art worlds.

Thanks to Tom's connections, Sarah's career took off, and she became a sought-after artist in New Zealand. She was even commissioned to create a mural for one of the city's largest buildings.

Tom was proud of Sarah's success and was happy to have been a small part of her journey. They had connected the dots, formed relationships and worked together for mutual benefit. They remained close friends and often collaborated on projects that helped the local community.

The two degrees of separation between Tom and Sarah had brought them together and had helped Sarah achieve her dreams. It just goes to show that in New Zealand, the spirit of community and collaboration can make anything possible.

If you can imagine yourself and your colleagues and peers as dots in the big matrix of the business world and if you connect the dots and make connections you will grow your network. You may have heard of six degrees of separation or two degrees of separation in New Zealand. Due to the New Zealand population being relatively low and multi-cultural everyone is more connected than you may think.

Larger countries such as the USA and UK consider that they have six degrees of separation and smaller countries such as New Zealand have two degrees of separation. How this works is that if you imagine yourself as the zero place holder and the people you know or have met as the first degree of separation. The people that they know or have met are two degrees of separation and are likely to have had some connection back to you.

Making connections everywhere you go closes the gap from two down to one and as your network increases the separation correspondingly decreases. Of course these connections can only be of value if we use them to build relationships that may benefit both parties.

In New Zealand, due to popular culture we think of us as having two degrees of separation, where in actuality, in some communities it may be more like three or four.

CHAPTER 2:
THE VALUE
OF BUILDING
RELATIONSHIPS

A small startup company called "GreenTech" that was founded by two young entrepreneurs, John and Jane. They had a passion for developing sustainable technology and wanted to make a difference in the world.

As their business grew, they quickly realised that they needed to build relationships with other businesses in order to succeed. They attended networking events and reached out to potential partners, but they found that many people were skeptical of their company's innovative ideas and untested products.

Despite these setbacks, John and Jane persevered. They knew that building relationships was crucial to their success, so they continued to seek out potential partners and invest time and effort in building a rapport with them.

One day, they met a business owner named Shona who shared their passion for sustainability. Shona was impressed by GreenTech's vision and saw the potential for a mutually beneficial partnership. She introduced John and Jane to other business owners in the industry, and before long, GreenTech was collaborating with several other companies on innovative projects.

Over time, GreenTech's reputation grew as a result of these successful partnerships. They became known as a company that was not only innovative but also reliable and trustworthy. Other businesses began to seek them out as partners, and before long, GreenTech was at the forefront of the sustainable technology industry.

The lesson that John and Jane learned was that building relationships is essential to success in business. By investing time and effort in getting to know others in their industry, they were able to build trust and establish a network of partners who could help them achieve their goals.

They also learned that having a passion for what you do and sharing that passion with others can be a powerful way to build meaningful relationships.

Shona, John and Jane continue to work together and are friends.

The foundation of business networking is building relationships. When you take the time to get to know someone, you are building a foundation of trust and respect. This trust and respect can lead to more business opportunities and referrals.

When you have a strong network of professionals who know and trust you, they are more likely to recommend you to their own clients and colleagues.

Building relationships is also important for personal growth. When you meet new people and learn about their experiences, you can gain valuable insights and knowledge that can help you grow both personally and professionally.

Networking events and conferences are a great way to meet new people and learn from their experiences.

CHAPTER 3:
THE VALUE OF
COLLABORATION

Two small businesses, a bakery and a coffee shop were located on opposite ends of a busy street. The bakery was struggling to attract new customers and the coffee shop was having trouble retaining customers for longer periods of time. One day, the owners of both businesses met at a local networking event and struck up a conversation.

They realised that by collaborating, they could both benefit. The bakery could provide the coffee shop with fresh pastries every morning and the coffee shop could offer a discount on coffee to customers who also purchased baked goods from the bakery. They agreed to give it a try and started working together.

The collaboration proved to be a success. The coffee shop's customers loved the fresh pastries from the bakery, and the bakery gained a new customer base thanks to the coffee shop's marketing efforts. The two businesses also shared marketing costs and increased their social media presence together, creating a stronger brand image.

As their collaboration grew, the two businesses started to brainstorm new ideas. They began hosting joint events, such as a coffee and pastry tasting, and worked together to create new products that combined their specialties. They also started to share their suppliers, resulting in lower costs for both businesses.

Word of mouth about their successful collaboration started to spread, and soon other businesses in the area began to take notice. More collaborations were formed, and the street became known for its thriving business community.

In the end, the bakery and coffee shop not only succeeded individually but also collectively, proving that collaboration and networking can be the key to success in the business world.

Collaboration is another key value of business networking. When you collaborate with other professionals, you can achieve more than you could on your own. Collaboration can lead to new business opportunities, new ideas, and even new products and services.

Collaboration can also help you overcome challenges and obstacles. When you work with others, you can draw on their strengths and expertise to help you solve problems and overcome obstacles. This can save you time and money, and help you achieve your goals more quickly.

CHAPTER 4: THE VALUE OF KNOWLEDGE SHARING

A young entrepreneur named Ruth, who had just started her own business, was was struggling to find clients and grow her company. She knew she needed to network and learn from others, but she wasn't sure where to start.

One day, Ruth attended a business conference where she met a seasoned entrepreneur named John. John had been in the industry for over 20 years and had a wealth of knowledge and experience. Ruth was hesitant to approach him, but she finally mustered up the courage to introduce herself and ask for his advice.

To her surprise, John was more than happy to share his knowledge with Ruth. He gave her tips on how to market her business, how to find clients, and how to manage her finances. He even introduced her to some of his own contacts who could potentially become clients for her.

As Ruth began to implement John's advice, she noticed a significant improvement in her business. She was able to secure more clients, increase her revenue, and even expand her business into new markets. She was grateful for John's help and realized the value of knowledge sharing and networking.

Ruth continued to attend business conferences and events, and she made it a priority to share her own knowledge with others. She realized that by helping others, she was not only giving back but also building relationships that could lead to future collaborations and partnerships.

Over time, Ruth became known as an expert in her industry, and her business continued to thrive. She never forgot the importance of networking and knowledge sharing, and she made it a core part of her business strategy.

In the end, Ruth learned that success in business isn't just about what you know, but who you know and how you share your knowledge. She was grateful for the generosity of others who had helped her along the way, and she was determined to pay it forward to the next generation of entrepreneurs.

Knowledge sharing is another important value of business networking. When you share your knowledge and expertise with others, you are not only helping them grow, but you are also building your own reputation as an expert in your field. When you are seen as an expert, you are more likely to be referred to others who need your services.

Knowledge sharing can also help you stay up-to-date on the latest trends and developments in your industry. When you attend networking events and conferences, you have the opportunity to learn from other professionals and stay current on industry best practices.

CHAPTER 5:
THE VALUE OF
GIVING BACK

A young entrepreneur named Louise, had recently started her own business, and had a great product and a passion for her work. However, she quickly realized that building a successful business required more than just hard work and determination.

Louise attended various networking events, hoping to connect with potential clients and partners. However, she found that most people were only interested in talking about their own businesses and what they could get out of the conversation.

One day, Louise met a successful business owner named John who took a different approach. Instead of talking about his own business, he asked Louise about hers and what she hoped to achieve. He listened carefully and offered helpful advice, introducing her to some of his contacts who he thought might be able to help her.

Louise was amazed at John's generosity and the time he took to help her. She left the event feeling grateful and inspired, realizing that there was more to networking than just trying to promote her own business.

Over time, Louise followed John's example and started to focus on giving back to others in her network. She attended events with the goal of helping others and building relationships, rather than just promoting her own business. She took the time to listen to others and offer advice when she could.

As a result, Louise found that her network grew stronger and more supportive. She met new people who became loyal clients and partners, and her business started to thrive. She realized that giving back to others wasn't just a good thing to do – it was also a smart business strategy.

Years later, Louise had become a successful business owner herself, and she looked back on her early days with gratitude for the lessons she learned about the value of giving back. She knew that without the support of others in her network, she would never have been able to achieve her dreams.

In the end, Louise learned that networking was

about building relationships and helping others, not just promoting her own business. By giving back to others in her network, she was able to build a strong foundation for her own success.

Giving back is a key value of business networking. When you give back to your community and help others, you are not only doing the right thing, but you are also building goodwill and a positive reputation for yourself and your business. Giving back can take many forms, such as volunteering your time, donating money to charity, or mentoring others.

Giving back can also help you build relationships and grow your network. When you volunteer your time or mentor others, you have the opportunity to meet new people and make new connections. These connections can lead to new business opportunities and referrals.

CHAPTER 6:
THE VALUE OF
DIVERSITY

In the bustling city of Stockton, there were three business professionals. The first was a young, ambitious entrepreneur named Emma. The second was a seasoned executive named Malik, and the third was a creative designer named Mei. They all had very different backgrounds, experiences, and perspectives.

Emma was born and raised in the city, and had always been fascinated by technology and innovation. Malik was originally from a small town in the south, and had spent his career climbing the corporate ladder in various industries. Mei grew up in a rural area and had always been passionate about art and design.

Despite their differences, they all shared a common goal: to build their network and grow their businesses. They decided to attend a networking event together, hoping to meet new contacts and learn from one another.

At the event, Emma immediately gravitated towards other young entrepreneurs who shared her passion for technology. Malik, on the other hand, connected with executives from similar industries and exchanged ideas about management strategies. Mei, however, found herself surrounded by a diverse group of people from different backgrounds and professions, and she struck up conversations with everyone she met.

As the evening progressed, Emma and Malik found themselves talking only to people who were similar to themselves, and they felt like they weren't gaining any new insights or ideas. Meanwhile, Mei was having a blast, meeting people from all walks of life and learning about their experiences and perspectives. She even got a few new design leads from people who were in unrelated industries.

At the end of the night, Emma and Malik were feeling discouraged and frustrated. They had gone to the event hoping to grow their businesses, but they felt like they had only spoken to people who were exactly like them. Mei, on the other hand, was feeling energized and excited. She had made new connections and learned so much from people who were very different from herself.

Over the next few months, Mei continued to attend networking events and build relationships with people from all different backgrounds. She discovered that the more diverse her network was, the more opportunities she had. She was able to collaborate with people from different industries and backgrounds, and she even started to see her designs in new and exciting contexts.

Emma and Malik, on the other hand, continued to network only with people who were similar to themselves, and they didn't see much growth in their businesses. They eventually realised that diversity was a key factor in building a successful network, and they started to seek out new and different perspectives.

Mei's willingness to embrace diversity and connect with people from all walks of life proved to be the key to her success. She realized that by surrounding herself with people who were different from herself, she was able to learn new things, gain new perspectives, and grow her business in ways she never could have imagined.

Emma and Malik learned that diversity was not only important, but essential to building a successful network in today's business world.

Diversity is another important value of business

networking. When you build a diverse network of professionals, you are exposing yourself to different perspectives and ideas. This can help you see things from a different point of view and come up with new and innovative solutions to problems.

Diversity can also help you reach new markets and expand your business. When you have a diverse network of professionals, you are more likely to be able to tap into new markets and attract a wider range of clients.

CHAPTER 7:
THE VALUE OF
AUTHENTICITY

A young entrepreneur named Lily had just started her own business and knew she needed to market her new business but was unsure where to start . She was excited to attend networking events to meet potential clients and partners.

However, she soon realized that the events were filled with people who seemed to be putting on a façade, trying to present themselves as something they were not.

Lily struggled with this because she believed in the value of authenticity. She knew that her business was built on her unique perspective and genuine passion for her work. She didn't want to compromise that by pretending to be someone she wasn't. Despite her initial doubts, Lily decided to stay true to herself at networking events.

She didn't try to impress others with fancy titles or exaggerated accomplishments. Instead, she shared her story, her vision, and her passion for her work.

At first, Lily was nervous that she would be seen as inexperienced or unimpressive. But to her surprise, people responded positively to her authenticity. They appreciated her honesty and enthusiasm, and they were interested in learning more about her business.

Through her authentic approach to networking, Lily was able to make meaningful connections with people who shared her values and believed in her vision. She found clients who were excited to work with her, and partners who were eager to collaborate with her.

Over time, Lily's business grew, and she became known as a leader in her industry. She was invited to speak at conferences and to participate in high-level discussions with other business leaders. Through it all, she stayed true to her authentic self, and people continued to respond positively to her genuine approach.

Lily learned that authenticity is a valuable asset in business networking. By being true to herself, she was able to build a strong network of like-minded individuals who supported her and helped her to achieve her goals. She knew that, no matter what challenges lay ahead, she could always rely on the power of authenticity to guide her forward

Authenticity is a key value of business networking. When you are authentic and genuine, you are more likely to build strong relationships based on trust and respect. Authenticity means being yourself and not trying to be someone you're not.

When you are authentic, you are also more likely to attract the right people to your network

ABOUT THE AUTHOR

Patrick K Teak

Patrick became an entrepreneur in the 1950s at a time when New Zealand was experiencing a growing economy with decreasing unemployment in the post-war years.

Starting out with his small custom made curtain business, he ventured into other soft furnishings and continued to grow his business.

After the 1984 election in New Zealand, Patrick moved his business to Melbourne and was joined there in 1990 by his brother Robert who joined him in business.

Patrick has been a member of many networking groups during his time in business and now in his retirement he can still be see offering advice to young entrepreneurs.

THE END